Wilmette Public Library

Photo by Joan Marcus

The set from the Manhattan Theatre Club production of "After-Play." Set design by Jim Youmans.

AFTER-PLAY

BY ANNE MEARA

★

DRAMATISTS
PLAY SERVICE
INC.

SPECIAL NOTE

Anyone receiving permission to produce AFTER-PLAY is required (1) to give credit to the Author as sole and exclusive Author of the Play in all programs distributed in connection with performances of the Play and in all instances in which the title of the Play appears for purposes of advertising, publicizing or otherwise exploiting the Play and/or a production thereof; the name of the Author must appear on a separate line, in which no other name appears, immediately beneath the title and in size of type equal to 50% of the largest letter used for the title of the Play. No person, firm or entity may receive credit larger or more prominent than that accorded the Author; and (2) to give the following acknowledgment on the title page of all programs distributed in connection with performances of the Play:

Originally produced by the Manhattan Theatre Club
with funds provided by the Harold and Mimi Steinberg Charitable Trust
on January 10, 1995.

SPECIAL NOTE ON SONGS AND RECORDINGS

For performance of the songs, arrangements and recordings mentioned in this Play that are protected by copyright, the permission of the copyright owners must be obtained; or other songs and recordings in the public domain substituted.

For my husband and partner,
Jerry Stiller

AFTER-PLAY was produced by Manhattan Theatre Club, Stage II (Lynne Meadow, Artistic Director; Barry Grove, Managing Director), in New York City, in January, 1995. It was directed by David Saint; the set design was by Jim Youmans; the costume design was by Jane Greenwood; the lighting design was by Don Holder; the sound design was by John Gromada and the production stage manager was Lisa Iacucci. The cast was as follows:

MARTY GUTEMAN	Merwin Goldsmith
TERRY GUTEMAN	Rue McClanahan
PHIL SHREDMAN	Larry Keith
RENEE SHREDMAN	Barbara Barrie
RAZIEL	Lance Reddick
EMILY PAINE	Rochelle Oliver
MATHEW PAINE	John C. Vennema

AFTER-PLAY transferred to Theatre Four in New York City, on May 2, 1995, under the auspices of Nancy Richards, Judith Resnick, Evangeline Morphos in association with Carol Ostrow. It was directed by David Saint; the set design was by Jim Youmans; the costume design was by Jane Greenwood; the lighting design was by Don Holder; the sound design was by John Gromada and the production stage manager was Pamela Singer. The role of TERRY was played by Anne Meara.

AUTHOR'S PRODUCTION NOTE

The director, designer and cast should be aware that this chic Manhattan-style restaurant is, in fact, a "restaurant" between two worlds, a sort of limbo and that, though they are not consciously aware of it, the three couples have died.

Raziel in the *Encyclopedia Judaica* is the Angel of the Unknown, the Angel of Mysteries.

AFTER-PLAY

SCENE ONE

A restaurant that appears to be a chic New York eating place, but is not. A large window is right of center, adorned with a seasonal Christmas wreath. A small bar is up left, next to the entrance door, down center is a large table with four chairs. A smaller table with two chairs is upstage under the window.

Raziel, the waiter, stands behind the bar. He looks out over the room and goes downstage to the table, where he straightens a place setting. He then crosses right, looks out the window and makes a sweeping gesture with his arm. Snow immediately starts to fall. Offstage we hear the sound of a car crash. Raziel does not seem surprised at this. He looks out the window and then looks at the door expectantly. Raziel then points to the door as if he is commanding someone to enter, then exits stage right just as Marty, Terry, Renee and Phil burst through the door.

MARTY.   God! Is everyone okay?
PHIL.   Shook up, I would say — a little shook up.
RENEE.   Cabdriver from hell.
MARTY.   The guy was a little out of it.
TERRY.   A little! He missed that truck by inches.
PHIL.   Close, but no cigar.
TERRY.   We're screaming and he keeps saying, "No problem, no problem...."
MARTY.   I think there was a language barrier.

RENEE. "No problem" is code for "drop dead, white devil."
(Marty groans in pain, bending over.)
TERRY. No. Oh, no, Marty. Please, no.
RENEE. Marty...?
TERRY. His back is out.
MARTY. *(In a contorted position.)* I'm fine.
TERRY. Do your stretches.
PHIL. Need a hand?
MARTY. *(On the floor doing stretches.)* It's loosening ... it's okay. It comes and goes.
TERRY. That idiot at the wheel didn't help.
PHIL. We should sue the bastard. Did anyone get his name or number?
RENEE. What difference? "Mohammad," "Mustapha," "Kalil" —
TERRY. Sounds a little racist, Renee.
RENEE. Me, racist? Don't be an ass. I marched in Selma, for God's sake.
PHIL. C'mon, forget it — we're here to enjoy. *(Marty groans.)*
RENEE. *(Standing over Marty.)* Lie on your back and pull your knees up to your chest, fetal position.
PHIL. Breathe into the pain, Marty.
MARTY. *(Follows Renee's instructions.)* Better — this is better. *(Raziel, the waiter, comes over to the group and stares at them.)*
TERRY. We're the Gutemans, party of four.
MARTY. *(To Raziel, explaining.)* Chronic back pain. *(Marty gets up with the help of the others.)*
RAZIEL. Oh, yes, we've been expecting you. I've always enjoyed your work.
MARTY. Really? Well, thank you.
RAZIEL. From Shakespeare to sitcoms, the gamut. You were the golden couple. Just let me take your coats. *(Raziel gets the coats and carries them offstage.)*
MARTY. What a sweet guy.
TERRY. Marty would think an ax murderer was sweet if he recognized him.
MARTY. Don't put me down, it's nice to be remembered.
TERRY. I wasn't putting you down.
RENEE. You know, that waiter could be the cabdriver's twin.

8

TERRY.   Yes! It's uncanny.

PHIL.   Dead ringer. *(Raziel returns. To Raziel.)* You don't happen to have a brother who's a kamikaze cabdriver, do you?

RAZIEL.   *(Smiling.)* I don't think so, but maybe a distant relative. *(Leading them to a table.)* Here we are.

MARTY.   *(Looking out the window.)* It's turning into a blizzard out there.

RENEE.   God, I'm still freezing. Come sit down, Marty.

TERRY.   *(To Marty.)* Any better, honey? *(Marty comes over to the table and sits, painfully.)*

MARTY.   Fine, fine — I'm used to it.

RENEE.   *(To Marty.)* Squeeze your buttocks.

PHIL.   Hey, I'm getting excited.

RENEE.   Shut up, it works.

TERRY.   Squeeze, Marty.

MARTY.   I'm squeezing, I'm squeezing.

RAZIEL.   May I get you something from the bar?

PHIL.   Believe it. A touch of the sauce, Marty. It'll straighten your back and stiffen your pecker. Booze, pronto, amigo.

RENEE.   Class act.

TERRY.   Those old theaters. We were packed in like sardines.

RENEE.   I was sitting right in a draft. *(To everyone.)* What should I have?

PHIL.   Can you make me a vodka martini, straight up?

RAZIEL.   Of course, sir. *(To Terry.)* Ma'am...?

TERRY.   White wine shpritzer for me.

PHIL.   And be sure to chill the glass.

RENEE.   I can't believe you're ordering a shpritzer.

TERRY.   I've reformed.

RAZIEL.   *(To Renee.)* Madam...?

RENEE.   God, if I have a martini I'll fall asleep. First bring me a glass of water or I'll die.... And a vodka Gibson, but no onions ... and a glass of rocks on the side ... and some menus would be nice.

MARTY.   What the hell. Scotch rocks for me.

TERRY.   Why not have a shpritzer?

MARTY.   I'm cold, okay? Scotch rocks, seltzer on the side. *(Raziel takes drink orders and hands Renee a menu.)*

9

RAZIEL. Would you care to hear the specials now?

RENEE. *(Handing Raziel back the menu.)* Please, we just got here, bring the drinks first.

PHIL. Make them all doubles.

TERRY. Doubles! No! We'll all be on the floor.

PHIL. You heard the lady, no doubles. Just mine.

RENEE. Have they got the air conditioning on, or what? *(To Raziel.)* This is ridiculous. Bring me my fur before I get pneumonia. Terry, do you want your coat?

PHIL. No, she wants your coat.

RAZIEL. Ma'am...?

TERRY. No, thank you. *(Raziel goes.)* Your blood is thinned from orange juice and palm trees.

PHIL. God, it's good to see you both.

RENEE. It's been what? — over three years.

MARTY. Friendship, that's what the holidays are all about. *(Raziel returns with Renee's fur coat.)*

TERRY. Three years ... God.

RAZIEL. *(To Renee.)* Did you need any help with your coat, ma'am?

RENEE. No help, thank you. I worked my ass off for every pelt.

MARTY. You're a riot, Renee.

PHIL. Quick. She's quick. *(Renee drapes her coat around her shoulders and sits.)*

TERRY. Did you know that each of those little minks was killed with an electric rod inserted up its rectum?

RENEE. No, I didn't. But now that I know, I can't wait to order dinner. Mmm, mmm — Yum, yum.

MARTY. Lay off the fur stuff.

TERRY. I'm just explaining the cruelty involved.

RENEE. Terry, my guilt list is so long, this mink isn't even a contender.

RAZIEL. My name is Raziel and I'll be your waiter this evening.

TERRY. "Raziel" — what a beautiful name.

RAZIEL. Thank you.

RENEE. Very exotic, very mysterious.

MARTY.   Where are you from, Raziel?

RAZIEL.   Queens. Just let me know when you're ready to order. *(Raziel goes.)*

PHIL.   Nice place. Is it new?

TERRY.   Supposed to be the "in" restaurant.

MARTY.   They say everyone ends up here after the theater.

PHIL.   Boy, we all go back together, don't we?

RENEE.   A hundred years.

PHIL.   Whoever thought we'd end up being the alta-cockers.

TERRY.   I keep looking behind me. What was that? What was that stuff all about?

RENEE.   We're not going to get melancholy, are we?

MARTY.   What stuff?

TERRY.   All that carrying on. All that stuff.

PHIL.   I think they call that Life.

RENEE.   My philosopher. Who knew he was so deep.

TERRY.   It's like this morning I was nine years old. It's now ten P.M. and I've gone through menopause.

RENEE.   Join the crowd, sweetheart. I had my last Tampax bronzed ages ago.

PHIL.   Renee, that's a little rough.

RENEE.   You have no idea, darling. *(Raziel comes with the drinks.)*

RAZIEL.   Shpritzer …

TERRY.   Oh boy, I'm parched.

RAZIEL.   … vodka Gibson, no onions, rocks side …

RENEE.   Don't spill a drop — I can't wait.

RAZIEL.   … vodka martini …

PHIL.   Nectar of the gods.

RAZIEL.   … and scotch rocks.

MARTY.   *L'chaim! (Raziel goes.)*

PHIL.   *(Making a toast.)* Wait, here's to us — old friends, old times, new times…

RENEE.   Cut to the chase. Health and a few laughs!

MARTY.   And let's not let it be so long between visits. *(They all drink.)*

TERRY.   *(Picking up the theater Playbill.)* So. What did you think? At the end there, I just wept.

PHIL. Not me.

RENEE. He never opens up, that's his problem.

PHIL. Just because I didn't burst into tears doesn't mean I didn't like a lot of it.

TERRY. Those scenes with the mother — God, those scenes just destroyed me.

MARTY. He was right on the button there. That was my mother to a "tee," even the apron.

RENEE. Naturally. He does his research.

PHIL. Research? On Marty's mother?

RENEE. *(To Phil.)* Comedian.

MARTY. That whole family, that was my family.

PHIL. The guy's a craftsman, no question.

TERRY. That last scene was transcendent.

PHIL. Brilliant choice.

RENEE. Loaded.

MARTY. Ending like that, back at the beginning, when they're all young ...

TERRY. And hopeful, looking to the future ...

MARTY. Not knowing what we know, that their dreams are going to be destroyed ...

TERRY. Devastating. Everybody gets dealt a different hand ...

RENEE. A potent device.

PHIL. Clever technique.

TERRY. Don't do that.

PHIL. What?

TERRY. Use those words. Technique. Device.

PHIL. We're not saying that the device wasn't moving, we're just saying it was a device.

TERRY. Well, it worked. *(Terry lights up a cigarette.)*

RENEE. You're not going to smoke.

TERRY. Renee, I smoke. You know I smoke. This is a designated smoking area. When I made the reservation, I asked for the smoking section, because, I smoke. I don't drink vodka Gibsons anymore, but I smoke.

RENEE. Go ahead. Kill yourself. Just don't blow in my area.

TERRY. *(Gets up.)* Switch with me, Marty.

MARTY. *(Reluctantly switches seats with Terry.)* What are you doing? C'mon, put it out.

TERRY. I'm blowing this way. Okay? *(Marty gets up and bends over, groaning.)* Oh, great....

MARTY. I told you, it comes and goes.

TERRY. Don't make me the bad guy....

PHIL. Not easy. I quit five years ago.

MARTY. Was that when you had the by-pass?

PHIL. Not just a by-pass, it was a quintuple.

RENEE. Show-off.

TERRY. *(Still upset.)* It's like we saw two different plays.

RENEE. Are you talking to me?

TERRY. That scene with the mittens — I just went to pieces.

RENEE. What mittens?

TERRY. When she's telling the daughter about her mother in the old country...

MARTY. That's the daughter's grandmother, who later comes back as a spirit....

TERRY. I'm telling this. The grandmother gave her these mittens when she came over from the old country ...

PHIL. See, that wasn't clear. The time frames changing, and the ghost thing ...

RENEE. He tried to cover too many bases.

PHIL. That whole immigrant scene, then the boys going off to war. Too much.

RENEE. That dead grandmother really got on my nerves.

PHIL. It was confusing. Murky.

TERRY. It was an epic, for God's sake. That scene with the mittens ...

RENEE. I don't remember any mittens.

TERRY. How could you not remember the mittens?! During the entire speech she's clutching the same mittens her mother gave her forty years earlier. Even though she doesn't mention the mittens, the scene is about what the mittens meant to her, because at the end, without saying a word, she hands the mittens to the daughter, and you know she's not just handing on mittens but a legacy, showing the continuity and connection between the generations.

RENEE. I felt that speech was very manipulative.

PHIL.   He was pushing our buttons.

RENEE.   Nostalgia is a cheap out.

TERRY.   Are you serious?

RENEE.   It was very well done, but I'm aware when my strings are being pulled.

MARTY.   I didn't get that at all.

TERRY.   You're saying you weren't moved?

RENEE.   Medium.

MARTY.   Medium?

RENEE.   Medium moved.

PHIL.   Renee's got a Richter scale for emotional involvement.

RENEE.   Cute. I was aware I was being moved, so when I'm aware that I'm being moved, I'm only medium moved.

TERRY.   I guess that makes me a pushover, according to you.

RENEE.   You have your opinion. I have my opinion.

MARTY.   I bought the whole thing, what do I know. *(Silence.)*

PHIL.   Listen, the whole evening was terrific. Just being here in the apple and seeing the both of you ...

RENEE.   Next time you come to the coast, we do the honors.

PHIL.   Absolutely. Marty, you lost weight.

MARTY.   Doctor put me on a new diet.

RENEE.   What did you do, Terry, you look fabulous. Nip and tuck? What?

TERRY.   Teeth. I had my teeth done. And therapy.

PHIL.   Therapy, at our age? That takes balls.

RENEE.   Does that stuff really work? I mean, half my friends have been going to one shrink or another for years ...

PHIL.   And they're still as fucked up as ever.

RENEE.   Can I finish a sentence, please? Oh, my God.

TERRY.   What?

RENEE.   My earring. I lost an earring.

PHIL.   Maybe you swallowed it.

RENEE.   Very funny! *(Phil and Renee get up, searching the table area. Terry gets up and looks under the table for the earring.)*

TERRY.   Maybe it's under the table. Wait I think I see it.

RENEE.   Where? Show me.

TERRY.   There ... by the base.

RENEE. No, no. That's part of the table. That's not my earring.

PHIL. Are you sure it didn't fall off in the cab?

RENEE. Shit, shit, shit.

MARTY. *(Upset, blows his nose.)* God help us. God help us.

RENEE. Forget it, Marty — they were cheap.

TERRY. Honey, are you all right?

RENEE. Keep squeezing, Marty.

MARTY. Deep stuff. I guess it hit some deep stuff in me.

TERRY. *(Crawling out from under the table by Marty's knees.)* I know, honey, painful — it was painful.

PHIL. *(Referring to earring.)* What did it look like?

RENEE. Like the other one.

MARTY. When the kid was saving up tinfoil to beat the Japs.

TERRY. When the girl gets her first period and she doesn't know what it is — Jesus, nobody ever told me ...

PHIL. A little too graphic for me.

RENEE. *(To Phil.)* Victorian.

MARTY. All those little details, they got to me. The decoder ring, the knickers ... all that stuff ...

RENEE. That's what I'm talking about, he took easy outs.

MARTY. Easy outs?

PHIL. Brand names, old radio theme music. Surefire triggers.

RENEE. That stuff never fails.

TERRY. Well, I'm a sucker then, because I fell for it.

PHIL. Forget it, honey — it's lost.

RENEE. Story of my life.

MARTY. I was there. In that kitchen. I almost sobbed out loud.

TERRY. I did.

MARTY. That milk bottle with the pennies the mother saved ...

TERRY. To pay the insurance man every week.

MARTY. And the kid sees his mother crying over the empty milk bottle, and he's too ashamed to say he took the money.

PHIL. That was a nice touch.

MARTY. Nice touch?! That was me!

TERRY. Are you all right?

15

PHIL.   I meant "nice touch" in the sense that most of us can relate to a similar incident.

MARTY.   I did that to my mother. I stole her kitchen money to buy a goddamn balsa wood airplane.

TERRY.   *(Calling to Raziel.)* Can we get some water here? *(Terry goes to the Bar. Raziel pours her a glass of water.)*

MARTY.   *(Upset.)* Never blamed me. She knew and she never blamed me. *(Terry brings the water to Marty.)*

TERRY.   Drink the water, honey.

RENEE.   We've all done things when we were kids. He struck a nerve, that's all.

TERRY.   How can you be so blasé?

PHIL.   *(To Renee.)* Ease up.

TERRY.   Stop making us feel like we've been had. *(Phil signals to Raziel.)*

RENEE.   I'm just separating the wheat from the chaff. People get fooled by shtick!

TERRY.   Shtick! There was no shtick. *(Raziel comes over.)*

RAZIEL.   Yes, sir?

PHIL.   Bring us another round. Give it a rest, Renee. *(Raziel goes.)*

RENEE.   Please. I've been in this business for half my life, and I know shtick when I see it. Funny shtick or sad shtick. Tonight I saw sad shtick.

TERRY.   You are unbelievable.

PHIL.   C'mon, we're getting silly. Renee doesn't mean to offend your ...

RENEE.   Guilty with an explanation — thank you, Phil.

MARTY.   It's not your fault. It's me.

TERRY.   Are you okay, honey?

RENEE.   *(To Phil.)* I don't need you to defend me.

MARTY.   I'm okay.

PHIL.   I wasn't defending.

RENEE.   Worse. Explaining. Don't explain me, please.

PHIL.   By me you're the Rosetta Stone.

MARTY.   I'm sorry, everybody.

RENEE.   What's that supposed to mean? Rosetta Stone?

TERRY.   Don't be sorry. You have nothing to be sorry about.

RENEE. Cryptic. That's what it means, cryptic.

TERRY. You saw a play and you were deeply moved. You have no reason to apologize to anyone.

RENEE. I'm a very direct person. I've never been cryptic. You're all full of shit.

MARTY. I'm sorry, I've got a very low threshold tonight. *(Raziel brings another round.)*

PHIL. Hey, this is what the theater is supposed to do, right? Stimulate controversy.

RENEE. Friends argue, no big deal. Here's to us. *(Renee toasts and everyone drinks. Marty gags on his drink.)*

MARTY. Going to the Men's, back in a minute. *(Marty goes.)*

PHIL. Is he okay?

TERRY. He's going through a very rough time right now.

RENEE. Medical?

TERRY. His cousin died.

PHIL. They must've been very close.

TERRY. It was his last cousin.

PHIL. I know what that is.

RENEE. What are you talking about? You have two cousins, a sister and a father.

PHIL. My father's dead. Has to be by now.

TERRY. Don't you know?

PHIL. He ran off to Canada with my Aunt when I was twelve. That's the last I heard.

RENEE. And he hasn't talked to his sister in twenty-five years.

PHIL. What do you say to a schizophrenic that you don't have to say twice?

RENEE. Mental illness is no joke.

PHIL. Especially if you're paying the hospital bills.

TERRY. Marty's father and mother both died in a car accident two years ago in Florida.

RENEE. God.

PHIL. At their age, they were still driving?

TERRY. Just Marty's mother. She was behind the wheel, his father was crossing the street.

PHIL. Awful.

TERRY. She swerved to avoid hitting a dog. Ran up on the

sidewalk just as his father stepped up on the curb. They were both killed instantly.

RENEE.   At least they were together.

TERRY.   Only in death. They'd gotten a divorce the month before.

RENEE.   They both lived in the same neighborhood?

TERRY.   Two blocks away from each other.

PHIL.   God.

TERRY.   That's what started us in therapy.

RENEE.   It would start anyone.

TERRY.   Well, that and our girls.

RENEE.   Susie and Polly? What's wrong with them? They're gorgeous.

TERRY.   They have a lot of anger. I was never there for them. Even when I was there, I wasn't there.

RENEE.   Stop beating yourself, you were a terrific mother.

PHIL.   You both had a career, for God's sake.

TERRY.   We were so busy trying to get rich and famous …

RENEE.   Sounds good to me.

TERRY.   You don't understand, Renee, I was hysterical in those days — screaming and yelling, getting plastered …

RENEE.   What is this? Confession? I thought you weren't Catholic anymore.

PHIL.   C'mon, you and Marty were wonderful parents.

TERRY.   We were a mess! Are you blind?

RENEE.   If this is therapy, get me another vodka Gibson.

TERRY.   Jesus, I'm sharing some insight with you! I used to be grandiose, overbearing …

PHIL.   You're too hard on yourself, Terry. She's reveling in atonement.

RENEE.   Stop flaunting your guilt, for God's sake.

TERRY.   I wasn't there, I'm telling you.

RENEE.   Kids always lay that on you. Catherine the Great probably got the same crap. "Mommy! Come play with us. Forget the horse!"

PHIL.   *(Laughs.)* That's a good one.

TERRY.   This is no joke. We never gave our kids boundaries …

RENEE.   "Boundaries"? What's that, more "therapese"?

TERRY. And they've suffered for it.

RENEE. Spare me from suffering kids! They don't know the meaning of the word. Pain? Heartache? I could write a book. I was alone. I was going through a divorce.

PHIL. She's right. A divorce is difficult.

RENEE. All my divorces were difficult! Not a dime did I get from either of those bums. I had two babies. I had a career.

PHIL. Take it easy.

RENEE. Don't tell me I wasn't a goddamn good mother! I had to hire a housekeeper and a cook for those kids. *(Marty returns to the table.)*

MARTY. Please, I'm sorry I upset everyone.

PHIL. We're fine. Nobody's upset.

MARTY. It's just that the play really got to me.

PHIL. Listen, the guy can write.

RENEE. Nobody lays track like he does.

PHIL. To the payoff. The man pays off.

MARTY. I think I'll have some soup.

TERRY. *(Sarcastic.)* "Track." "Payoff."

PHIL. We're paying the guy a compliment.

TERRY. I hate it.

MARTY. They're only taking a professional view.

TERRY. I resent that elitist attitude.

MARTY. I'm going to ask if they have any soup.

RENEE. Don't be ridiculous, no one's being elitist.

TERRY. Ivory tower elitist attitude.

PHIL. Sometimes it comes out caustic — she doesn't mean it.

RENEE. That's two. Caustic and cryptic.

PHIL. There were poignant moments in the play, but a lot of it isn't clear. It gets ... *(Raziel comes over.)*

RAZIEL. We have some late-night specials, if you'd care to hear them.

RENEE. I'm starving. What would I like?

RAZIEL. Tonight we have a Blackened Bluefish with wild rice, a medallion of *Veal Provençal*, and the pasta of the day is a *Fettucini Verdi*.

TERRY. What, exactly, wasn't clear, Phil?

PHIL.   Well, there were a lot of obscure allusions ...

TERRY.   What was obscure?

RENEE.   The *fettucini* — does it have mushrooms?

PHIL.   She can't eat mushrooms.

RAZIEL.   There are a few morel mushrooms mixed in with florets of broccoli, sun-dried tomatoes and leeks, done in a fennel cream sauce.

RENEE.   Too heavy.

TERRY.   What was obscure, Phil?

PHIL.   Take the speech the daughter gives at the end ...

TERRY.   An epiphany!

MARTY.   Hold it down.

TERRY.   A goddamn epiphany!

RENEE.   Maybe to you. To me it was *chuffa*.

PHIL.   Well, I wouldn't say *chuffa*. Convoluted.

TERRY.   *Chuffa!* My God, it was poetry.

PHIL.   *(To Raziel.)* Can he make eggs?

RAZIEL.   How would you like them, sir?

PHIL.   Scrambled. Dry.

TERRY.   What, exactly, did you find to be *chuffa?*

MARTY.   The waiter wants to know what you want.

TERRY.   Pasta. I want the pasta.

RENEE.   I'll tell you what the *chuffa* was. All that stuff about the snows melting and the veins of the world.

TERRY.   Transformation! Snow changing into water, the veins of the world, how we're all connected.

RENEE.   *(To Raziel.)* The medallions of veal — is that heavy?

RAZIEL.   Yes.

TERRY.   It was a metaphor, for God's sake.

PHIL.   Could've fooled me.

MARTY.   Do you have any soup?

RAZIEL.   Cauliflower au gratin.

TERRY.   A simple metaphor. The seasons of life, renewal, growth ...

RENEE.   Bring me the veal.

TERRY.   I can't believe you're ordering veal.

RENEE.   It's light. It's tender. Bring me a few lemon wedges on the side.

20

TERRY.   Do you have any idea how they get veal?

RENEE.   Not really, but I'm sure you do.

TERRY.   They take the baby calf from its mother's womb and shove it into a small dark stall and tie it up so it can't lie down. Then they force feed the calf water to soften up the meat, that's what makes it tender. And there the poor little creature stands, without its mother, all alone, in filthy excrement, starved and terrorized until it is brutally slaughtered at the age of two months.

RENEE.   *(Holding her crossed wrists up to Raziel.)* Book me! I'm guilty.

TERRY.   You want the veal, order the veal.

RENEE.   And have a cross burned on my lawn? No thanks. *(To Raziel.)* Bring me the *fettucini verdi,* but kill the mushrooms. Humanely, if possible.

RAZIEL.   Yes, ma'am. *(To Marty.)* Sir...?

MARTY.   Soup and a house salad.

PHIL.   And you can bring us another round.

MARTY.   Not for me. *(Raziel goes.)*

RENEE.   What did you order?

PHIL.   Scrambled eggs.

RENEE.   Loaded with cholesterol.

TERRY.   Always with an "opinion" on everything.

RENEE.   Was that to me?

TERRY.   A goddamn masterpiece and you're too blind to see it. The veins of the world is us. What's so obscure about the veins of the world?

RENEE.   "Veins of the world" was a lot of airy-fairy shit.

TERRY.   *(Mumbling.)* Typical. Pearls before swine.

RENEE.   What's that?

MARTY.   The play meant a lot to us, Renee.

RENEE.   Well, there's no need to be rude.

TERRY.   Yes there is. There's a definite need to be rude.

PHIL.   We're all tired. *(Silence. Lights fade down to blue as the turntable turns — lights up again.)*

SCENE TWO

MARTY.   Toby? Toby Fenner?

PHIL.   Last week. He was having dinner at the Gerbers' house, he went to the bathroom and, evidently, collapsed.

TERRY.   My God!

MARTY.   Toby Fenner.

RENEE.   I thought you knew.

PHIL.   They couldn't get the door open.

TERRY.   What door?

PHIL.   To the bathroom. When he fell, his body blocked the doorway inside the bathroom, so they couldn't get it open.

RENEE.   Toby was a big man.

PHIL.   Massive heart attack. Must've been instantaneous.

TERRY.   How did they get in?

PHIL.   Who get in?

TERRY.   The bathroom. How did they get the door open?

PHIL.   I don't know.

RENEE.   Sheila told you. They had to take it off the hinges.

PHIL.   They had to take it off the hinges.

MARTY.   God.

RENEE.   When the paramedics came, they took the door off the hinges.

MARTY.   My God, poor Toby.

TERRY.   Toby, Toby, Toby.

MARTY.   Nobody told us.

PHIL.   We thought you knew.

TERRY.   How could we know, if nobody told us?

RENEE.   It was in the papers.

PHIL.   The L.A. papers.

RENEE.   Well, that's the papers. L.A. papers are papers.

MARTY.   So, how would we know if it was in the L.A. papers?

RENEE.   They didn't have it in *The Times*?

TERRY.   He just told you it wasn't in the New York papers.

MARTY. Maybe it was. I don't read the obits.

TERRY. Someone should've called us.

RENEE. What difference. It's over.

TERRY. I can't believe you wouldn't pick up a phone and …

PHIL. We didn't think. It all happened so fast.

RENEE. He was cremated right away.

TERRY. (Loud.) We were very close. You should have called us!

MARTY. Hold it down.

RENEE. Don't yell at me.

PHIL. It was an oversight, Terry. Renee and I were calling a list of relatives, someone else was supposed to call you.

TERRY. Well, they didn't.

MARTY. So full of life … such a zest for living …

TERRY. Greatest sense of humor …

PHIL. Everywhere, dropping like flies.

MARTY. This is some express train.

TERRY. Just this past year: Chuck McKean, Felicia Croydon, Lillian Mossman …

MARTY. It's a *blitzkrieg.*

RENEE. Lillian!

TERRY. It was some shock.

PHIL. Lillian Mossman's dead!

RENEE. Lillian! I didn't know.

TERRY. It wasn't in the L.A. papers?

RENEE. That was unnecessary, Terry.

TERRY. (Laughing.) Not really.

PHIL. Terrific girl, Lillian — so athletic …

MARTY. An "A" tennis player.

TERRY. Brilliant mind.

RENEE. And style, the woman had style. What was it, cancer?

TERRY. Varicose veins.

RENEE. This is a joke?

TERRY. I'm telling you, she went in for varicose veins, the anesthetist opened the wrong nozzle. End of story, casket closed.

MARTY. They're suing the hospital.

RENEE. Good luck! Those AMA boys stick together.

TERRY.   Closer than the Vatican.

PHIL.   Malpractice bastards.

RENEE.   I'll keep my varicose veins, thank you.

MARTY.   It's all a crap shoot.

TERRY.   It boggles the mind. So fast, so fast.

RENEE.   Faster than the speed of light, kids.

PHIL.   C'mon, you're as old as you feel. Age is a number.

RENEE.   You believe that, you'll believe Oswald was the lone assassin.

MARTY.   Everything's falling apart.

TERRY.   When was it together?

PHIL.   Hey, what is this? Nothing's falling apart. We're still here. C'mon, it ain't over 'til the fat lady sings. *(Phil toasts and drinks, the others do not join him. Raziel arrives with the food.)*

RAZIEL.   *Fettucini verdi* ... scrambled dry ... and cauliflower *au gratin* with house salad.

MARTY.   Good, I really wanted this soup.

RENEE.   What is this — a pogrom?

RAZIEL.   Your *Veal Provençal* will be here in a moment. Sorry for the delay.

RENEE.   I had changed my order to the *fettucini* without the mushrooms.

PHIL.   That's right, I heard her.

RAZIEL.   Sorry, ma'am, my mistake. I'll have the *fettucini* for you in a few minutes. *(Raziel goes.)*

RENEE.   This always happens to me. Was this difficult? What was so difficult? I cancelled the veal and took the *fettucini*. You heard me.

PHIL.   They heard you in Cucamonga. *(Marty laughs.)* Never fails.

TERRY.   What never fails?

RENEE.   Cucamonga. One of those funny names. People laugh because it has a "k" sound.

TERRY.   This is a comedy rule?

PHIL.   No, it's just a funny word. Like Toluca Lake, La Brea Tar Pits.

TERRY.   Toluca Lake isn't funny.

MARTY.   La Brea Tar Pits doesn't have a "k" in it.

RENEE. That's Phil's alta-comedy philosophy. Too many USO shows over the dam. Nobody laughs at that crap anymore.

MARTY. I laughed.

RENEE. That's what I mean.

MARTY. Is that a put-down?

PHIL. Renee just means it's a generational thing.

RENEE. Once again, Phil, thank you for signing for me.

TERRY. When I was a kid I couldn't stand the sound of those comedians' voices. "Well, I wanna tell ya"...

MARTY. I loved them. They made us laugh. My parents would stop fighting and they would laugh.

PHIL. Those guys were my gods. That's what made me want to be in the business.

RENEE. C'mon, you wanted to get laid.

PHIL. Of course.

MARTY. I miss those days.

TERRY. I miss now.

RENEE. I miss my *fettucini.* Where the hell is my *fettucini?*

TERRY. Take half of my *fettucini,* and when yours comes I'll take half. Here, I'll pick out the mushrooms.

RENEE. No, absolutely no! It's not important. This isn't about *fettucini. (Getting up.)* Back in a minute. Want to join me, Terry?

TERRY. I'm okay.

RENEE. God, this place is freezing. *(She leaves.)*

PHIL. That waiter's a little flaky. Everyone heard her order the *fettucini.*

MARTY. Mistake. Everyone makes mistakes.

TERRY. Phil, is everything okay?

PHIL. Couldn't be better.

TERRY. You heard her. She said this isn't about *fettucini.*

MARTY. He said everything's fine, Terry.

TERRY. I can ask, can't I?

PHIL. No problem. She's had a rough year, that and the holidays. You know.

TERRY. How are her kids?

PHIL. Everyone's fine. Brian's working as a second A.D. over

25

at Universal.

MARTY.   Doesn't his father work there?

PHIL.   No, that's Heather's father. Brian's dad was in real estate.

MARTY.   Was...?

PHIL.   Terrible thing. He got caught up in that Savings and Loan mess and dove off a bridge onto the Harbor Freeway.

TERRY.   Selfish bastard. Poor Brian. There's nothing worse.

PHIL.   Forget "poor Brian," he's fine. Both of those little shits are doing just fine. Waiter! Let's get a refill here. *(Phil goes to bar, gives Raziel his glass and walks over to table.)*

TERRY.   Aren't you being a little hard on them?

PHIL.   She gives them everything and they spit on her. Heather was living in a dump in West Hollywood. Renee moved her out of there and bought her a condo in Pacific Palisades.

MARTY.   That's a beautiful area.

PHIL.   Two hundred and fifty grand beautiful, plus furnishings.

TERRY.   That's exorbitant.

PHIL.   On top of that, Renee sends Brian and his wife to Maui for two weeks while she baby-sits the grandchildren. *(Raziel brings Phil his drink and goes.)* Ah, not a moment too soon.

TERRY.   How old are the twins now?

PHIL.   They're ten. Then Brian up and divorces his wife and runs off with Ula Thornbourg.

MARTY.   Ula Thornbourg!

TERRY.   The Swedish bimbette.

MARTY.   I love her!

TERRY.   The one woman in Sweden who can't act.

MARTY.   She's wonderful. She was great in that French movie ... it was a remake ... what was it?

TERRY.   *Liaisons Dangereuse?*

PHIL.   *Diabolique?*

MARTY.   No.

PHIL.   *Murmur of the Heart?*

MARTY.   No.

26

TERRY. *Babar!* Who cares.

MARTY. No. Anyway, I found her very moving. The language barrier was hardly any problem for her.

TERRY. You said it was in French, for God's sake.

MARTY. The other actors were in French — she played a Swedish mute.

TERRY. What difference. Brian left Renee's grandchildren and ran off with an immigrant.

PHIL. The twins live with their mother in Studio City, and guess who's picking up the tab?

TERRY. Renee, she never lets on. Shit.

PHIL. And here's the capper. She's paying the rent, and this putz forbids her to see her own grandchildren.

TERRY. Toughest job in the world, being a mother.

PHIL. The whole parent deal is a bum rap.

TERRY. Motherhood is harder. From the first tremor in the womb, to the day they put you on a respirator, it's a series of aftershocks. *(Silence.)*

MARTY. I still say, Ula Thornbourg is a deeply moving, luminous talent. *(Lights fade down to blue as the turntable turns — and lights up again.)*

SCENE THREE

Renee comes back to the table.

RENEE.   What? A wake? A *shiva*? What? *(Terry gets up, runs to Renee and embraces her.)*
TERRY.   Renee, I'm so sorry.
RENEE.   No, I was out of line. That scene with the mittens was a good scene.
TERRY.   Brian and Heather ...
MARTY.   Phil told us about the kids.
RENEE.   Thank you, Phil, for turning a pleasant reunion with friends into a discussion of disasters.
MARTY.   It's my fault. I asked how they were doing.
RENEE.   And he told you.
PHIL.   What am I supposed to say? They've made you sick. They've given you a mastectomy, for God's sake.
TERRY.   Renee...!
RENEE.   Better yet, Phil. Now we can discuss my mutilation.
MARTY.   Renee, I'm sorry.
RENEE.   It's okay. I'm squeaky clean now. I even had a reconstruction job.
PHIL.   My gal's as good as new. Better.
RENEE.   As usual, Phil is a little over the top, but I'm fine.
TERRY.   You look great.
RENEE.   Not really. But my new breast looks better than my face.
TERRY.   Sorry about the kids.
RENEE.   Go, be a mother and get kicked in the heart.
MARTY.   Maybe if you could all sit down and talk.
RENEE.   Talk! Don't be an ass. Who sits down and talks?
TERRY.   He's just saying it's really helpful when everyone communicates and listens to each other. Marty and Susie and Polly and I have gotten so much ...
RENEE.   These kids don't listen. They don't care zip about what we went through to give them what they've got.

PHIL. Ungrateful cockers.

RENEE. You think Phil's son gives a shit about him?

PHIL. Okay, Renee.... That's enough.

RENEE. He's in therapy ... no offense, Terry ... blaming Phil for divorcing his mother, blaming his mother for dying of cancer and blaming me for everything.

PHIL. The boy has deep emotional problems....

RENEE. Boy! Adam is over thirty.

PHIL. They think it's, whaddya call...? Manic depression.

RENEE. Bipolar. They call it bipolar now.

TERRY. We all have issues with our parents that go back to childhood, Renee....

PHIL. Could be a chemical-imbalance thing.

RENEE. I have no issues! My mother was a saint! She washed, cleaned and cooked for all of us and my father who thought he was artistic. He was so artistic he died of cirrhosis of the liver. She broke her fingers sewing brassieres in a sweat-shop while I took care of my little brothers.

PHIL. Don't upset yourself, honey....

RENEE. I took care! I was responsible! And I'm still taking care. I took care of my kids. Who else was going to do it? Both of their fathers were losers. I was the one who had to buy Brian the car for high school. I was the one who scrimped to give Heather the acrobatic, ballet and tap! I picked up the tab for everyone. Phil, get me a drink!

PHIL. Waiter...! Waiter...!

MARTY. It's Raziel. *(Raziel comes over.)*

RAZIEL. Yes, sir, the *fettucini* is on the way.

RENEE. Cancel the *fettucini*. Bring me another drink.

RAZIEL. But the *fettucini* is almost ...

RENEE. Listen, Raffael, I hate *fettucini*, okay? I want a vodka Gibson. No onions?

RAZIEL. No problem, ma'am. *(Raziel goes.)*

MARTY. His name is Raziel.

RENEE. Who gives a shit. *(Long pause.)* I miss my grandkids.

TERRY. They miss you too, Renee.

RENEE. They hate me. Their mother poisons their minds against me. My own daughter hit me.

PHIL. Don't get into this.

TERRY. Heather?!

RENEE. I'm telling you, she hit me with a colander.

TERRY. That's over the line, Renee — that's inappropriate behavior.

RENEE. Who are you, the therapy police?

MARTY. What's a colander?

TERRY. A strainer for food.

RENEE. Not just a strainer, a metal strainer.

TERRY. I can't believe Heather hit you. She's a wonderful kid.

RENEE. She's so wonderful, she's working as a receptionist for some holistic dentist.

TERRY. She's finding her way.

RENEE. She's educated and she's talented, and she's flushing her life down the tubes. Believe me, there's no second chances in this rat race. You've got to be aggressive — go in for the kill and watch your back.

TERRY. What did you do?

RENEE. What do you mean, what did I do?

TERRY. You said she hit you.

RENEE. And to you that means I did something, right?

PHIL. Don't get into this, girls.

RENEE. There are no girls here, Phil! Girls do not have wrinkles and mastectomies and children who hate them.

PHIL. Don't upset yourself.

RENEE. Maybe your by-passes have given you glaucoma.

MARTY. Can I get you some coffee, Renee, or a cappuccino?

RENEE. Terry seems to think I pulled a Joan Crawford on my daughter.

TERRY. I didn't mean it to sound like ... *(Raziel comes and gives Renee her vodka Gibson and goes.)*

RENEE. I did nothing, unless you want to count the fact that I re-did her entire kitchen. Of that I'm guilty.

PHIL. You didn't eat anything, honey. Let me order you some soup.

RENEE. Shut up. I re-did Heather's entire kitchen, get the picture? A new stove plus microwave, subzero refrigerator, sink with disposal, new cabinets, tile lunch counter, new floors and paint job.

TERRY.   I'm not questioning your generosity ...

RENEE.   Heather wanted the appliances to be in Avocado, and I told her that Stainless was the way to go. So, I ordered Stainless. After they installed everything she said that she had wanted the Avocado but that I didn't listen to her, that I never listened to her, and I said I did listen to her and that Avocado was Valley-tacky, that Stainless had more class and would last longer, and that she really had no color sense and would one day thank me. Then she hit me with the colander.

TERRY.   Jesus.

PHIL.   The girl has deep emotional problems.

MARTY.   Parents and kids. Tough.

PHIL.   We're talking Menendez here. *(Silence. Lights fade down to blue and up again. No more turntable moves.)*

SCENE FOUR

Everyone is sitting in same position as Scene Three. Terry, looking at Renee, softly starts singing an old girls' camp song.

TERRY.   *(Sings.)* Cookie, cookie, listen while I sing to you,
Cookie, cookie, you're a part of campfire too.
(Renee joins in.)
  Anyone can make a bed, anyone can sew,
  But it takes a cookie, to make us eat and grow.
  So cookie, cookie, listen while we sing to you.
  We really mean it —
  Listen while we sing to you.
  This is the last time —
  Listen while we sing to you.
  I guess we fooled you —
  Listen while we sing to you.

MARTY.   *(Rising.)* Excuse me. Nature calls.

PHIL.   *(Also getting up.)* Me too. Hey, I never showed you my scar. *(Phil starts to unbutton his shirt.)* They slit me open from here to here ... *(He indicates sternum to navel.)* Like a baked potato. *(Marty and Phil go to the Men's Room.)*

TERRY.   Phil looks good.

RENEE.   He could lose a few.

TERRY.   He's crazy about you.

RENEE.   I make him laugh. He drinks too much and he eats too much, and he's a very considerate lover ... so was Marty, as I remember.

TERRY.   *(Laughing.)* God, I'd almost forgotten that.

RENEE.   Jurassic memories.

TERRY.   The Village ... *chianti* bottles ... youth ...

RENEE.   You were a lousy roommate ...

TERRY.   You were worse ...

RENEE.   *(Laughing.)* You stole Marty away from me ... you snared him in your *shiksa* goddess net.

TERRY. *(Laughing.)* You tossed him to me like a party favor.

RENEE. Who the hell can remember? We were all twelve years old.

TERRY. You had hordes of tumescent guys salivating in the wings.

RENEE. "Tumescent" — now, there's a word to wrap your tongue around.

TERRY. *(Laughing.)* God, how I envy you.

RENEE. Envy! Be serious. My body parts are slowly disintegrating, my children are candidates for the Hitler Youth, and I have moments of despair that would terrify you. If it weren't for Phil ... I'd be dead.

TERRY. You're strong, you're resilient — you're everything I wanted to be ...

RENEE. Don't do that to me. Don't put me in some superwoman box ... I'm a quivering custard, like everyone else. I just talk loud. I never had my fifteen minutes. I skirted the area, but I never had my fifteen minutes.

TERRY. You had ardor, you had lustiness, you had desire ...

RENEE. Oh, that. We were young. I didn't know what the hell I was doing ... screwing my brains out ...

TERRY. *(Emotional.)* I never had that ...

RENEE. It's exhausting. Why? You and Marty are fine, aren't you? You're his life, you know.

TERRY. Yes, yes, he's wonderful. I love him, I'm just getting to know him. He's such a sensitive ... we're learning so much about each other in thera ... *(She breaks down.)* I'm sorry.

RENEE. Give yourself a break.

TERRY. *(Emotional.)* Passion! I never had passion! Now it's too late.

RENEE. Don't be an ass. If Marty's slowing down, do what everyone does, get a vibrator.

TERRY. It's not Marty — it's me. Toxic nuns, sins of impurity. I'm strangling in ancient rosary beads, I'm trapped in some eternal Lent.

RENEE. You've been married forever. In all that time didn't —?

TERRY. Yes, yes. It was ... pleasant. It was ... I don't know...

Marty's too good, too kind. I need some fantasy Neanderthal who'll treat me like … like …

RENEE.   Dirt?

TERRY.   Yes.

RENEE.   Whatever works.

TERRY.   It's disgusting.

RENEE.   It's only disgusting when other people do it. Use your imagination — get Marty a motorcycle jacket; wear an old negligee that he can rip off you…. Dress-up is fun — Phil loves it.

TERRY.   You are hilarious.

RENEE.   I'm serious. You have a great guy.

TERRY.   I know.

RENEE.   Well, cherish him.

TERRY.   Yes, yes, I know …

RENEE.   Be sure the motorcycle jacket is genuine leather …

TERRY.   *(Laughing.)* Okay …

RENEE.   With a lot of zippers …

TERRY.   Right.

RENEE.   And handcuffs are not out of the question …

TERRY.   *(Embracing Renee.)* Absolutely. *(Marty and Phil come back to the table.)*

MARTY.   Did you know that Phil was clinically dead on the operating table for four minutes?! *(Renee and Terry are laughing loudly.)*

PHIL.   No joke, it was touch and go there for a while. *(Lights fade down to blue and up again.)*

SCENE FIVE

PHIL. So, this undertaker is preparing a body for a funeral. He pulls back the sheet, and the guy's got the biggest schlong he ever saw. He's amazed. He calls his assistant over …"Max, c'mere. I want to show you something." Max comes over, and the undertaker says, "Did you ever see anything like this in your life?" Max looks, and says, "What's the big deal. I got one like that." The undertaker says, "Oh, c'mon Max. Don't kid around." Max says, "No, I really got one like that." Undertaker says, "Max, be serious. You don't have…" Max says, "I'm not kidding. I got one exactly like that." Undertaker says, "Really? You got a schlong *that big?*" Max says … "Oh, … you're talking *big,* I'm talking DEAD!" *(They all laugh.)*

TERRY. God, there's Emily and Mathew.

MARTY. Where?

TERRY. That table in the back. They're getting up.

RENEE. Friends?

TERRY. For ages. They're heading over here.

MARTY. What do we say?

TERRY. We say hello. It's been a year.

RENEE. What?

TERRY. Their son died of leukemia.

MARTY. Twenty-nine years old. *(Emily and Mathew come over. Emily leads the way.)*

RENEE. God, that's the worst. *(Emily has had too much to drink.)*

EMILY. Terry, Marty, I see you found the best after-hours joint in town!

MARTY. You guys look great.

TERRY. Join us.

MATHEW. Thanks anyway, we just ate. *(Emily grabs a chair from a nearby table and sits.)*

EMILY.   You twisted my arm. Maybe an after-dinner drink.

MATHEW.   We just had an after-dinner drink.

EMILY.   *(Laughing.)* Can't fly on one wing. Matt is so solemn. He has all these rules — don't you, Matt? *(Raziel brings a chair over for Mathew.)*

TERRY.   Renee and Phil Shredman, Emily and Mathew Paine.

RAZIEL.   *(To Emily and Mathew.)* Yes sir? Ma'am?

MATHEW.   Club soda or seltzer.

EMILY.   Oh, what the hell. An Irish coffee.

MATHEW.   You just had an Irish coffee.

EMILY.   And now I'm having another Irish coffee.

MATHEW.   Waiter, make mine a scotch on the rocks. *(Raziel goes.)*

EMILY.   Is this a contest?

MATHEW.   What's the occasion?

RENEE.   Phil and I are just in from the coast, so ...

PHIL.   We hadn't seen Marty and Terry for about three years, so ...

RENEE.   He was asking me, I believe. We haven't seen each other for three years, so Terry and Marty took us to the theater.

EMILY.   We just saw a bomb.

MATHEW.   Pretty dismal.

EMILY.   Supposed to be one of those "black comedies." A few laughs, a few tears, lots of death and screaming.

MATHEW.   Not very funny.

EMILY.   The second act was better.

MATHEW.   After your double-martini intermission.

EMILY.   Whatever it takes. So, what did you see?

TERRY.   A wonderful play: "Jamie, We Hardly Knew You".... Oh, God, I'm sorry.

EMILY.   It's okay.

MATHEW.   No problem.

RENEE.   What?

MATHEW.   We lost our son a year ago.

EMILY.   His name was Jamie.

TERRY.   I am so stupid.

EMILY.   No, we talk about it. It's okay.

RAZIEL.   *(Raziel brings the drinks.)* Scotch rocks and Irish coffee. *(Raziel goes.)*

RENEE.   Terry told us. Leukemia. I know what that is. My brother died of leukemia. He lived in Vegas.

PHIL.   I don't think we should go into that right now.

RENEE.   I wasn't "going into it." I was just letting Emily and Mathew know that I understand what a horror leukemia is. I was with my brother for the last two weeks of his life. You wouldn't get it, Phil, you hadda be there. And if memory serves me correctly, you weren't there.

PHIL.   Here we go.

RENEE.   It's no accident that Nevada has one of the highest leukemia and cancer rates in the country.

MARTY.   I didn't know this.

PHIL.   The testing. All that nuclear stuff.

RENEE.   Anyway, back in the sixties or seventies they made some John Wayne movie in Nevada on an old testing site that was radioactive.

MARTY.   What movie was this?

RENEE.   Some movie. *The Conquest.*

PHIL.   *The Conqueror.*

RENEE.   *The Conquest.*

PHIL.   *The Conqueror. The Conquest?*

RENEE.   What difference?! The thing is, over ninety people in that cast and crew died from leukemia or cancer.

TERRY.   Horrible.

MARTY.   Can they prove it?

RENEE.   Get serious. The CIA boys whitewashed the whole thing.

EMILY.   It wasn't leukemia.

RENEE.   Yes it was. They've documented cases. The deaths were caused...

EMILY.   My son didn't die from leukemia — it was AIDS.

TERRY.   AIDS! But I thought ...

MATHEW.   We didn't tell anyone.

MARTY.   God, Matt, I'm sorry.

MATHEW.   We took Jamie up to the country house at the end. We didn't want to put everyone through that.

EMILY. We didn't want to put ourselves through that, you mean.

PHIL. A plague, a terrible plague.

MATHEW. Em's right. We just couldn't face the ... I don't know. It was a shock. Out of the blue ...

EMILY. Out of the blue? I don't think so.

RENEE. How long had he been...?

PHIL. Renee ...

RENEE. Sorry, I was just wondering ...

EMILY. How long he'd been sick or how long he'd been gay?

MATHEW. He was diagnosed HIV two years before he died.

TERRY. Two years. My God, to carry that burden around for ...

EMILY. It wasn't a burden, it was my son.

TERRY. No, no, of course. I meant ...

MATHEW. Our son.

EMILY. Matt's been overcompensating lately.

MATHEW. I'm not overcompensating.

EMILY. He's really been great about it. He even wears his little red ribbon ... don't you, Matt. Show them your little red AIDS ribbon. *(She goes through his pockets.)* Where's your little red ribbon? Oooh, he forgot his little red ribbon.

MATHEW. *(Pushing her hands away roughly.)* You had to have that second Irish coffee.

TERRY. Emily, I wish I'd known.

EMILY. Really — why?

TERRY. I could've been there for you, I could've ... I don't know.

MATHEW. Nobody knows.

EMILY. *(Singing loudly.)* De trouble ah seen, nobody knows my sorrow. Nobody knows de trouble ah seen ...

MATHEW. *(Loudly.)* Shut up!

EMILY. Oops! Sorry, I get carried away. So, what exactly would you have done, Terry? Send me books, like my sister-in-law did? She sent me cartons of books: Louise Hay, Kubler-Ross. Courses upon courses in fucking Miracles.

RENEE. Are there any groups that you can go to?

PHIL. Renee ...

EMILY. Excuse me?

PHIL. Renee.

RENEE. Stop saying "Renee" like that. You're treating me like an outpatient.

EMILY. Groups? Like what? Community theater? PAC groups? What?

MATHEW. Give it a rest, will you?

RENEE. I'm sorry.

EMILY. Me too. No, we do. We go to groups. Matt drags us to every goddamn grieving gay group there is.

MATHEW. It helps.

EMILY. Who? Matt loves these groups. He gets to give testimony. He gets to make it up to Jamie and openly "share." "My name is Mathew, and I am the father of a dead gay boy who had AIDS."

MATHEW. *(Emotional.)* Christ, will you stop....

EMILY. Aw, look, he's so bereaved ... the star mourner!

MARTY. Emily ...

EMILY. They love him, all those lost infected men. He's their aging macho champion.

TERRY. How about a cup of coffee, Emily.

EMILY. Sounds great. Irish, if you don't mind.

MATHEW. Time to go, I think.

EMILY. You get off on it. Instant redemption for years of living on a distant planet.

TERRY. Em, c'mon, come to the Ladies' with me.

EMILY. I don't have to go, okay? I'm happy here with my Irish. You should appreciate that, Terry. You're Irish, aren't you? As I remember, you used to toss a few back in the old days. Right, Matt? Remember those New Year's parties with Marty and Terry when she'd sing old Catholic girls' school hymns, while her kids would try to get her to stop? *(Laughing.)* Your kids were so embarrassed, trying to pick you up off the floor, dragging you into the bedroom. God, I'll never forget the look on Marty's face. Remember that, Marty? Remember those drunken parties, where Terry used to humiliate you in front of all of us? God, it was hilarious.

MARTY.   Don't do this, Em.

MATHEW.   Sorry, Terry, it hasn't been easy.

TERRY.   It's okay. I understand.

EMILY.   You don't understand shit! None of you understand anything! When I buried my boy, he weighed sixty-five fucking pounds.

MATHEW.   I'll get our coats. *(Mathew goes.)*

EMILY.   *(Really losing it.)* Yeah, get the coats. Bastard! Where was he when Jamie wanted to talk to him? Shoving him into sadistic Little League games. Jamie wanted to go to Pratt he says, Sure, Jamie, but go to Babson first. Get that MBA, then you can paint all you want. Is that a riot! Now my husband is the Gay Men's Health Crisis Poster boy! *(Screaming after Mathew.)* Aren't you, Matt! Aren't you the understanding straight-father fantasy of every queen in town! *(Emily falls off her chair.)*

RENEE.   Pick her up, for God's sake.

TERRY.   Help her, Marty.

MARTY.   C'mon now, Emily …

EMILY.   Don't touch me. Don't anyone touch me. *(Raziel comes over.)*

RAZIEL.   May I help?

RENEE.   The husband went to get the coats. *(Raziel, in a deft, practiced move, gently lifts Emily up.)*

EMILY.   Get away from me! You're a gay boy, aren't you? You're a gay boy whose father was out to lunch, like my boy's father….

RAZIEL.   Take it easy, ma'am, it's okay. *(Mathew returns with the coats. He drapes Emily's coat over her shoulders.)*

PHIL.   I'll walk you out.

MATHEW.   No, we're fine.

EMILY.   Nobody's fine — nobody. *(To Raziel.)* Goddamn fag! You all killed my boy, you hear me?!

MATHEW.   *(Upset, shakes Emily hard.)* Stop it! I'm sorry. We … my wife … we lost our son.

RAZIEL.   Yes.

EMILY.   I'm sick, Matt. I want to go home.

MATHEW.   We are. We're going home, Em. *(Emily and*

Mathew head toward the door.)
RAZIEL. *(To Emily and Mathew.)* Everything's going to be all right now. *(Emily and Mathew exit. Silence.)* Can I get anybody anything?
MARTY. No. We're terribly sorry.
TERRY. We apologize.
RAZIEL. No problem. It happens all the time.
RENEE. All the time?
RAZIEL. More and more. *(Silence. Phil is standing, looking out the window. Renee, Terry and Marty are seated at the table. After a long silence.)*
MARTY. I think we could all use some coffee.
RENEE. Cappuccino sounds good. Phil? *(Phil doesn't respond.)* Phillie, get away from the window — you'll freeze to death. *(Phil comes back to the table. He is visibly distraught.)*
PHIL. Goddamn shits, all of them. They suck the life out of you. You bust your balls to make it and they mock you. They spit on everything you worked for....
RENEE. Sweetheart, we thought we'd order some coffee....
PHIL. *(To Marty and Terry.)* No. Those people, those friends of yours? They're finished. They bought the farm because of that schmuck kid of theirs.
TERRY. The boy died, for God's sake!
MARTY. A tragedy. Devastating.
PHIL. And why? Because he got the business end of some poison penis in a leather bar.
MARTY. Jesus, Phil...!
TERRY. How can you say such a horrible thing! I knew that boy. He was a good boy, a loving boy....
PHIL. These kids are all the same. They drag you down to hell with their scorn and resentments, their diseases and their drugs....
RENEE. Phil, don't — don't upset yourself.
TERRY. That boy was suffering! His parents didn't hear him, his parents didn't want to hear him....
MARTY. Don't start this. Don't lecture him.
RENEE. *(To Terry.)* Who anointed you judge and jury?
TERRY. *(To Marty.)* I'm not lecturing ... why do you turn

on me...?!

PHIL.   They sabotage us, they wreck us.... My God, every time, every single time something good has happened for me, he fucked it up. *(Calling to Raziel, holding out his empty glass.)* Let's get a refill here! *(Raziel comes on, takes Phil's glass and leaves.)*

RENEE.   *(Goes to Phil, embraces him.)* Don't let him get to you, honey.

TERRY.   We're the parents, Phil, we're the problem, not the kids.

RENEE.   *(To Terry.)* You don't know anything! Phil's series gets nominated for an Emmy, his son gets busted —

PHIL.   No, c'mon — forget that ...

RENEE.   *(To Terry.)* The night Phil was honored as "Man of the Year," Adam overdosed.

PHIL.   It was just an award. No big deal.

RENEE.   A prestigious award, given by your peers.

PHIL.   All right, all right, not important. What the hell. It was an award, okay? I was being given a goddamn award. Is that a crime? I'm no monster, I'm just a gagwriter who got lucky. I'm a human being, a father, I care ...

RENEE.   Of course you do, sweetheart.

PHIL.   Three o'clock in the morning, police stations, emergency rooms, stomach pumps — I was there ...

RENEE.   He was there.

PHIL.   I did everything for him. I got him gofer jobs at the studio. He met all the greats in the business. When he was a toddler, I'd bring him to the set. He sat on Benny's lap, for God's sake....

RENEE.   You treated him like a prince, Phillie.

PHIL.   And he pisses on me.

MARTY.   Ah, Phil, it isn't easy. None of this is easy....

RENEE.   He ran up over fifteen thousand on Phil's credit cards. *(Raziel brings Phil a fresh drink and leaves.)*

PHIL.   Enough of this dreck. Over the dam, under the bridge.

TERRY.   He doesn't want to get away with it, Phil. It's a cry for help.

MARTY.   Will you stop, already?

42

TERRY.   I know what this is. I went through it with the girls....

RENEE.   What is this — an encounter group?

MARTY.   Do you have to dredge up every bit of personal misery that we've been through?

TERRY.   I know your pain, Phil — I've been there. It's important to get in touch with these feelings, no matter how....

RENEE.   Please. Stop with this pain business. We all know pain. Who are you, the martyr of the universe?

TERRY.   You can't bury all this emotion under a scab. It's still there, festering....

RENEE.   A scab is scar tissue. People our age have a lot of scar tissue. If we didn't have scabs, we'd bleed to death.

MARTY.   You can't force therapy on people.

TERRY.   Stop undermining me!

MARTY.   Stop trying to convert him.

RENEE.   Once a gentile, always a gentile.

PHIL.   What are we doing here? I'm sorry, let's get off this stuff. Old news.

TERRY.   I was just letting Phil know that I care....

PHIL.   I know that, kid, it's okay. It's over. We move on.

TERRY.   Just sharing my feelings with people I love....

RENEE.   Do us a favor — don't love us so much.

PHIL.   Listen, it's my fault. Going into that whole *megillah* ...

TERRY.   Just trying to help, to show empathy for Phil's upset....

MARTY.   Teresa, enough already!

RENEE.   You know, you're addicted to suffering. You're a "pain" junkie.

TERRY.   Thank you, Renee, for being so understanding.

RENEE.   This whole evening is turning into an extended root canal. *(Silence.)*

PHIL.   What we all need is a good laugh. Better than your therapy, Terry.

RENEE.   Phil's right. Who needs tragedies? We get enough of that every day.

MARTY.   Laughter is healing. That guy wrote a book about it. He laughed himself right out of a hospital bed.

TERRY.   The man who wrote that book died.

RENEE.   Well, before he died he had a few laughs. Which is better than picking at scabs.

PHIL.   Okay ... moving along. Did you hear about the Israeli and the Arab sitting next to each other on a transatlantic flight? It was nighttime, they had their shoes off and the blankets over them. And the Arab says, "My dear Jewish friend, would you mind going back and getting me an orange juice, since you're sitting on the aisle?" The Israeli says, "Not at all, my Arab brother," and he goes and brings back the juice for the Arab. The Arab drinks down the juice, then laughs and says, "While you were gone I spit in your shoe." The Israeli sighs and says sadly, "Spit in the shoe, piss in the juice — when will it end?"* *(Marty and Renee and Phil are convulsed at the joke.)*

RENEE.   Oh, God ...

PHIL.   What's the matter?

RENEE.   I'm peeing!

MARTY.   Hilarious. *(Long pause.)*

TERRY.   I read a story in the paper about an actress who was filming a scene in a movie in Taiwan.

RENEE.   Why do I feel this is going to be a sad story?

TERRY.   In this scene her children are taken away from her....

RENEE.   Bingo...!

TERRY.   And this actress, she was a Chinese actress, said how painful it was because the same thing happened to her as a child when she was taken away from her mother....

RENEE.   Vietnamese.

TERRY.   What...?

RENEE.   The actress was Vietnamese.

TERRY.   That's not the point.

RENEE.   Well, I read the article, and if you're telling it you should get it right.

TERRY.   It's not the point. It's a story about loss. The woman

---

* Depending on the political climate, other jokes may be substituted.

44

could be anything: Chinese, Vietnamese, Siamese ... whatever.

PHIL.   Sure, just have the shirts back by Thursday. *(Marty laughs, Renee smiles, enjoying it. Terry stares at Phil.)*

TERRY.   I can't believe you said that.

PHIL.   What? C'mon, it was a joke.

TERRY.   From when — 1955?

RENEE.   Earth to Terry. The man was trying to cheer us up.

MARTY.   He didn't mean anything.

TERRY.   You laughed.

MARTY.   It was funny.

TERRY.   Not if you're Chinese.

RENEE.   She was Vietnamese.

TERRY.   Who cares about her?! I'm not talking about her. Doesn't anyone get it?

MARTY.   Don't make a thing out of this.

TERRY.   I'm talking about mother and child, and he's making jokes like Mickey and Morty and Dicky and Drecky.

MARTY.   Give the guy a break.

PHIL.   I was wrong, okay? I was ... whaddya call it ... politically incorrect, right?

RENEE.   No need to grovel, Phil.

TERRY.   I'm talking about the pain of separation, the gaping void that can never be filled!

RENEE.   I thought that you and your kids were closer now, with all that therapy, getting in touch with all that festering.

MARTY.   It really has helped, Renee. Polly and Susie and Terry and I, we've broken down a lot of barriers. We're learning to be more ...

TERRY.   I'm not talking about them! *(Terry gets up and runs to the Ladies' Room.)*

RENEE.   God, what was that?

PHIL.   It was just a joke.

MARTY.   It's not you. It's her mother.

RENEE.   *(To Phil.)* Her mother died when she was a kid.

MARTY.   Suicide.

PHIL.   Boy, oh boy.

RENEE.   Suicide! This, I didn't know.

MARTY.   Her mother had always been a nervous woman....

RENEE. To say the least.

MARTY. Those days that's what they called it, "nerves." Terry and her Dad had gone to a Chinese restaurant to get take-out, and when they got home they found the mother dead on the bathroom floor.

PHIL. I'm sorry. I am so sorry.

RENEE. It's not your fault, Phil.

MARTY. How were you supposed to know?

PHIL. *(Upset.)* Sometimes I go overboard. I didn't mean to —

MARTY. It's okay, it's okay.

PHIL. It's not okay! You don't understand, I almost did the other joke…. *(Phil gets up.)*

MARTY. Phil …

PHIL. My God, I almost did the "one from column A, one from column B" joke…! *(Phil goes to the Men's Room. Silence.)*

RENEE. *(Explaining, simply, sadly.)* Comedy is his life. *(Lights fade down to blue and up again.)*

SCENE SIX

Renee and Marty are alone at the table.

RENEE. It's getting colder in here. It's not my imagination.

MARTY. *(Calling to Raziel.)* Is there any way to turn the heat up? *(Raziel comes over.)*

RAZIEL. I really apologize. There's been a breakdown in the system.

RENEE. We know — family values, crime, earthquakes and floods. Meanwhile my fingers are turning blue.

MARTY. Do you have an electric heater or something? *(Phil comes back to the table.)*

RAZIEL. I'm afraid not, sir. But let me offer you and your friends an after-dinner drink, compliments of the management.

PHIL. Count me in. Courvoisier, coffee on the side.

RENEE. Kalhua and coffee.

MARTY. Just a decaf.

RAZIEL. Anything for the other lady, sir?

MARTY. Make it two decafs. *(Raziel goes. Silence.)*

PHIL. It's a different world today.

RENEE. Stick that in a fortune cookie.

PHIL. All different. Different everything. Sex, music, jokes. God, I hate their jokes.

RENEE. They hate our jokes.

PHIL. We had jokes. Set-up, rhythm, punch line. They just dribble on. What is that?

RENEE. Different generation. Different shtick.

PHIL. I feel like an alien without a map.

MARTY. It's like being homesick.

PHIL. Why can't I get what they're laughing at?

RENEE. They're laughing at us. We're the crap they grew up on.

PHIL. We're not crap! Don't write us off. We were good. We came through, we pulled ourselves out of shit and we came through.

RENEE. Phillie, honey, it's okay …

PHIL. I just don't want to end up being their joke. *(Silence.)*

MARTY. *(To Phil.)* Remember the stage shows when we were kids? The movie would end and those big velvet curtains would close, then you'd hear the band playing and like magic the orchestra pit would rise up in a flood of blinding light.

PHIL. And the comic would come out. He'd just stand there onstage, all alone. In charge.

RENEE. Well, not all of them were in charge.

PHIL. In total command. Secure. And he'd take his time, going easy, very conversational, because he knew that the pay-off was coming, that moment of victory when he'd kill.

MARTY. And we'd wait for him to deliver us, we'd wait for him to make us laugh.

PHIL. And the belly roars would wash over him like mother's milk.

RENEE. Please, those guys were barracudas, don't romanticize them.

MARTY. Yes, yes! Then he'd bring out the gorgeous blonde with a body that was out of control …

PHIL. Oh, yeah … the legs that went from here to there and back again…

MARTY. And then they'd do the bits…

PHIL. Doctor! Doctor! I haven't spoken to my wife in three years!

MARTY. Really, why's that?

PHIL. I didn't want to interupt. Doctor! Doctor! What's this terrible rash?

MARTY. Have you had it before?

PHIL. Yeah.

MARTY. Well, you've got it again!

PHIL. Doctor! Doctor! Nobody pays any attention to me!

MARTY. Next! *(Phil and Marty are convulsed.)*

RENEE. Pathetic, you're both pathetic.

PHIL. God, it was another universe …

MARTY. It was shiny and bright. It wasn't cracked linoleum and toilets in the hall, and mothers and fathers beating each other. It was everything, it was ... possibilities.

RENEE. It was show business, Marty.

MARTY. It saved me. *(Silence. Terry comes back to the table.)*

PHIL. *(To Terry.)* Terry, I'm sorry.

TERRY. Stuff comes up, Phil. Not your fault.

MARTY. Are you okay, honey?

TERRY. Fine, fine.... So, what did I miss?

RENEE. The boys were getting nostalgic over the old stage show comedians.

TERRY. *(A happy memory.)* God. Those marvelous picture palaces! My mother would take me when I was little. She'd hold my hand during the movie and weep and I'd weep with her. Just the two of us and those people up on the screen. I loved them, those silvery pretenders who made life real... I hated the comedians. *(Raziel comes over with the drinks and the coffee.)*

RAZIEL. Would anyone care to see our dessert menu?

PHIL. No thanks, I'll wait 'til they make the movie. *(Raziel smiles, everyone else laughs.)*

RENEE. Better. That's the "A" material. *(To Raziel.)* I need something sweet. Bring me something sweet. *(Raziel goes.)*

MARTY. I'm on Micronase.

PHIL. Diabetes. Welcome to the club.

RENEE. After fifty, it's all a paste-up job.

MARTY. I keep thinking that I should have gotten everything "in order," you know ...

RENEE. In order? What? Your whole life?

TERRY. People do that. They keep family histories in Bibles and albums ...

RENEE. New England people did that. They kept diaries and had reunions around the hearth with a lot of holly and shit.

MARTY. I'd just like to make some sense out of it all.

PHIL. What sense? There's no sense. Everyone does their turn and gets off, so the next slob can screw up.

RENEE. Thank you, Phil, for giving meaning to my life. *(Silence.)*

TERRY. I think I saw Nellie Kramer on the street the other day.

MARTY. Nellie! We were on the road with her once.

PHIL.   She's an actress, Nellie Kramer?

MARTY.   She was a wonderful actress.

TERRY.   Years ago, she did "Ariel" in *The Tempest.* The Times said she was magnificent.

RENEE.   So...?

TERRY.   I think I saw her sitting on the sidewalk ...

MARTY.   Sitting...?

TERRY.   This old woman — well, probably our age, who could tell — she was wrapped up in a filthy blanket, sitting over a hot-air grate, holding a paper cup...

RENEE.   A bag lady...?

MARTY.   Nellie Kramer, a bag lady?

TERRY.   I don't know. I think it was Nellie Kramer. I went over to put some money in her cup and she looked up at me and laughed.

RENEE.   Did she recognize you?

TERRY.   She didn't say "God bless you" or whatever those people say when you give them something. She just laughed and gargled something that sounded like, "How's it goin', kid?"

RENEE.   They're everywhere. It's getting worse.

PHIL.   Some of them are very aggressive.

TERRY.   It was Nellie Kramer. I know it was Nellie Kramer.

MARTY.   How could that happen?

RENEE.   How does any of this happen?

PHIL.   Hey, you make a turn in the road, things go wrong ... who knows.

TERRY.   I'll never forget her eyes — they lit up when she saw me. No resentment, no envy, just laughing, "How's it goin', kid?" Then I gave her a twenty and she started to cry.

RENEE.   Maybe she was working you for a fifty.

PHIL.   Renee ...

RENEE.   She said *The Times* gave her a great review.

MARTY.   What a waste.

PHIL.   Who can figure.

TERRY.   I'll never forget her eyes.

MARTY.   There's got to be something else.

TERRY.   Other generations seemed to have more purpose.

Pioneer women baked bread, had sixteen children and forged through the Donner Pass.
RENEE.   Where they froze to death or ate each other. *(Raziel comes with the dessert tray.)*
RAZIEL.   Tonight we have Baked Alaska, *crème brûlée*, chocolate torte, fresh raspberries or lemon sorbet.
RENEE.   Terry, share the torte with me?
MARTY.   God, I love chocolate cake.
TERRY.   I'll have a taste.
MARTY.   Nothing for me.
PHIL.   What the hell, give me the crème brûlée. *(Raziel goes.)*
RENEE.   Not even a taste, Marty?
MARTY.   I'm on the Micronase.
RENEE.   So's Phil.
PHIL.   It evens out.
TERRY.   Why can't we all just grow old and accept the seasons of life?
RENEE.   "Seasons of Life" — sounds like an airport novel.
PHIL.   Too "Biblical" for me.
RENEE.   "Seasons of Life," "Ages of Man" — whatever you call it, we all end up with a tag on our toe.
TERRY.   How can you be so negative? Three quarters of the world believes in an afterlife.
RENEE.   Naturally. They're starving in deserts, brushing flies from dead babies, waiting for Allah to save them.
TERRY.   Not only Third World people believe in...
RENEE.   If you want to believe in some cosmic Disneyland, go ahead. Let all the mothers of all the dead kids from all the wars believe that their little boys are up there, doing a *hora* with Buddha, or Christ ... or ... Shirley. Whoever.
MARTY.   How can you be so sure you're right?
RENEE.   Who's sure? I expect nothing.
TERRY.   I know there's something more....
PHIL.   I'm leaving my eyes.
MARTY.   Even on PBS, they had a show about reincarnation.
RENEE.   God, you mean I get to do this again?! No thank you, I'd rather live in Cleveland. *(Phil and Marty laugh.)*
MARTY.   "Cleveland" is funny — the "k" sound, right?

PHIL. Not if you've played there.

TERRY. There is more, there is some other … something.

RENEE. You think when your friend Nellie what's her name dies, she's going to get a feathery hug from compassionate angels? You think her life of misery and despair is going to be made up to her? I … don't … think so. *(Raziel brings the drinks.)*

MARTY. You know my mother and father died in a car accident in Florida. And right after we got the phone call telling us they died …

TERRY. Two pigeons flew onto our apartment balcony …

MARTY. They just circled around us and then flew away!

RENEE. In opposite directions, I bet.

MARTY. What…?

TERRY. It's okay, honey.

PHIL. This is getting depressing.

RENEE. Brushing my teeth is depressing.

MARTY. At least you *have* teeth.

RENEE. That's what you think. *(Raziel comes over and gives out the desserts. Lights dim down to blue and up again. In the dim light Marty groans and goes to lie down on the floor.)*

PHIL. Oh, Marty. What is it your back?

TERRY. Do your stretches, honey.

SCENE SEVEN

Terry and Renee are at the table, Marty is on the floor doing his back exercises, Phil is standing, looking out the window. Raziel clears away the dessert dishes and puts them on a nearby service table.

RENEE.   That chocolate thing was the best. Marty, you missed a piece of nirvana.

RAZIEL.   We're closing in a few minutes, so this will be "last call."

TERRY.   *(To Marty.)* Maybe another drink would help it.

MARTY.   *(In pain.)* No, no, this is good. It's easing up.

RENEE.   *(To Phil.)* Still snowing?

PHIL.   Deep drifts. Can't even see the fire hydrant. Where the hell are we?

RENEE.   I don't really know this neighborhood.

TERRY.   Nobody knows this neighborhood.

RAZIEL.   *(To Phil.)* Can I get you something from the bar, sir?

PHIL.   An aquavit, straight.

RENEE.   Nothing for me. *(Raziel goes over to Marty.)*

RAZIEL.   If you'll allow me, sir, maybe I can help.

MARTY.   It's chronic — comes and goes. *(Marty gets up.)*

RAZIEL.   May I? *(Raziel runs his hands up and down Marty's spine. Marty relaxes.)*

MARTY.   That's remarkable!

TERRY.   No pain?

MARTY.   *(To Raziel.)* Thank you! God, you really have the touch. Isn't that something?

RENEE.   He could put those Park Avenue boys out of business.

TERRY.   Thank you, Raziel.... Marty ...

MARTY.   What...? *(Terry gestures for Marty to give Raziel some money.)* Oh. Right. Of course. *(Marty reaches for his wallet.)*

RAZIEL.   Not necessary. No problem, no problem. *(Raziel goes to get the aquavit for Phil.)*

MARTY.   *(Doing a little dance.)* Hey! I'm not bad. C'mere, kid…. *(Marty grabs Terry.)*

TERRY.   *(Laughing.)* What! You're crazy…. We haven't done this in years. *(Marty and Terry dance and sing a song like "I Was Lucky,"* then end with a deep dip.)*

PHIL.   Together again, "The Gutemans"!

TERRY.   God! What a night … so much stuff….

MARTY.   I don't want it to be over.

TERRY.   No. It was just so … fast…. *(Terry emotional, holds Marty.)* I want to call Polly and Susie.

MARTY.   *(His arm around Terry.)* It's too late to call the girls, honey.

TERRY.   I know.

RENEE.   Why's everyone so morose? I had a great time.

TERRY.   Great time! We were all screaming at each other.

RENEE.   Screaming's okay. It's part of the deal.

TERRY.   *(To Phil and Renee.)* I'm sorry. I was an ass, I was overbearing, arrogant, and —

RENEE.   All of the above. Forget it. *(Holds her arms open to Terry. They embrace.)*

PHIL.   Hey, friendship, that's what it was all about, wasn't it? — the upsets, the good times, the whole ball of wax. *(Phil hugs Terry and Terry goes to Marty and embraces him.)*

RENEE.   Aw, Phil … you're sweet. Did I ever tell you that? *(They embrace.)*

PHIL.   Not lately.

MARTY.   So great being with you guys.

RENEE.   Maybe I will have another drink.

PHIL.   Raziel…!

MARTY.   He already gave "last call."

PHIL.   It ain't over 'til it's over. *(Raziel comes over carrying their coats.)*

RAZIEL.   Yes, sir…?

---

* See Special Note on Songs and Recordings on copyright page.

PHIL.   Can we get one more drink here?

RAZIEL.   Sorry, sir, we're closing now.

RENEE.   Forget the drink, I'm fine. I just want ... something....

RAZIEL.   *(Handing Renee her earring.)* I believe you dropped this.

RENEE.   My earring. I thought it was lost.

RAZIEL.   *(Laughing.)* Nothing is lost, ma'am.

RENEE.   Raoul, you're an angel. *(Raziel has handed out the coats and hats by now. He is still holding Terry's cape. Renee has her coat with her.)*

MARTY.   I really loved that play.

TERRY.   So sad ... but happy parts, too....

RENEE.   The old sweet and sour....

PHIL.   I didn't get all of it....

RENEE.   We got what we got. *(Raziel is holding Terry's cape. She takes it and puts it on.)*

TERRY.   Well. "Our revels now are ended." *(Terry turns to Raziel.)* Aren't they? *(Raziel smiles.)*

RENEE.   Oh yeah. Dream stuff, that's us. "Rounded with a sleep..." C'mon, Phillie.

PHIL.   No, not yet.

RENEE.   *(To Raziel.)* We weren't too awful, were we?

RAZIEL.   You were perfect. *(Raziel takes Renee's hands and kisses them.)*

MARTY.   *(To Raziel.)* Could I have just a taste of that chocolate cake?

RAZIEL.   I'm afraid the kitchen is closed. *(Marty goes to the service table where dessert dishes are piled and takes a plate with some cake crumbs.)*

MARTY.   Just a taste, okay?

RAZIEL.   Help yourself.

MARTY.   *(Savoring the crumbs.)* Good. This is so good.

RENEE.   C'mon, Phillie, it's over — time to go.

PHIL.   Not yet. I didn't hear the fat lady....

RENEE.   He never knows when to get off.... *(We hear a rich*

deep soprano voice singing, Maria Callas "Je veux vivre dans ce reve,"
from Gounod's Romeo et Juliette.*)

PHIL.   Now, that's an exit. *(Phil takes Renee's arm and they go out the door. Marty dips his finger into the chocolate and holds his finger out to Terry. She licks the chocolate from Marty's finger.)*

MARTY.   *(To Raziel.)* Thank you for everything. I hope we weren't too demanding.

RAZIEL.   No more than anyone else. You were fine.

TERRY.   Thank you, Raziel.

RAZIEL.   Safe trip. See you next time.

TERRY.   You're kidding...?

MARTY.   *(Still licking his fingers from the cake crumbs.)* Really...?

RAZIEL.   *(Takes the cake plate from Marty.)* Absolutely.

TERRY.   — Yes! *(Raziel smiles. Terry and Marty go out the door. Raziel closes the door, walks over to table, sits D.S.L., picks up Phil's acquavit glass, toasts the audience and drinks as the deep soprano voice fills the room. Lights fade to black.)*

CURTAIN

END OF PLAY

* See Special Note on Songs and Recordings on copyright page.

PROPERTY LIST

Men's coats (PHIL, MARTY)
Fur coat (RENEE)
Cape coat (TERRY)
Drinks (RAZIEL)
Cigarette (TERRY)
Matches or lighter (TERRY)
Handkerchief or tissue (MARTY)
Pitcher of water (RAZIEL)
Glass of water (RAZIEL)
Dinner plates with food (RAZIEL)
Dessert tray (RAZIEL)
Dessert plates with food (RAZIEL)
Earring (RAZIEL)

SOUND EFFECTS

Car crashing